THE PRESIDENCY OF

ROOSEVELT

Leading from the Bully Pulpit

BY EMMA CARLSON BERNE

CONTENT CONSULTANT
RICK MARSCHALL
MEMBER, ADVISORY BOARD
THEODORE ROOSEVELT ASSOCIATION

COMPASS POINT BOOKS
a capstone imprint

Compass Point Books are published by Capstone,
1710 Roe Crest Drive, North Mankato, Minnesota 56003
www.capstonepub.com

Editorial Credits
Melissa York, editor; Becky Daum, designer and production specialist;
Catherine Neitge and Ashlee Suker, consulting editor and designer

Photo Credits
AP Images, 7, 53; Corbis: 19, 39, 41, 47, 49, 58, Bettmann, 29, 44, Hulton-
Deutsch Collection, 13; Library of Congress, cover, 5, 9, 11, 14, 17, 18, 21,
23, 24, 27, 30, 33, 34, 42, 46, 50, 57, 59; National Archives and Records
Administration, 37; Red Line Editorial, 55; Thinkstock, 31
Art Elements: Shutterstock Images

Library of Congress Cataloging-in-Publication Data
Berne, Emma Carlson.
  The presidency of Theodore Roosevelt: leading from the bully pulpit / by
Emma Carlson Berne.
      pages cm.—(Greatest U.S. presidents)
  Includes bibliographical references and index.
  ISBN 978-0-7565-4925-1 (library binding)
  ISBN 978-0-7565-4933-6 (paperback)
  ISBN 978-0-7565-4941-1 (ebook PDF)
1. Roosevelt, Theodore, 1858–1919—Juvenile literature. 2. Presidents—
United States—Biography—Juvenile literature. 3. United States—Politics and
government—1901–1909—Juvenile literature. I. Title.
  E757.B48 2015
  973.91'1092—dc23 [B]   2014007012

Printed in the United States of America.
3529

TABLE OF CONTENTS

President,
UNEXPECTED

On the day before the president of the United States died, Theodore Roosevelt was halfway up a mountain. This might have been an unusual place for a vice president, but it was not an unusual place for Roosevelt. The vigorous outdoorsman relished long hikes, rides, and climbs, and at that moment, he was completely satisfied. He and his friends had just climbed to the peak of the highest mountain in the Adirondacks. They had descended partway and stopped for dinner. Roosevelt was just about to bite into a sandwich when a messenger appeared

Theodore Roosevelt was known throughout his life for his love for the outdoors.

on the trail below with a yellow telegram in his hand. As soon
as he saw the telegram, the vice president knew just what it
contained—bad news.

President William McKinley had been shot and wounded
September 6, 1901, in Buffalo, New York, by an anarchist
named Leon Czolgosz. Vice President Roosevelt had stayed
by the president's bedside for four days, and the president
had seemed to be mending. Roosevelt left with his family for
a planned Adirondack vacation, partly to reassure a nervous
nation that McKinley was getting better.

But now, eight days after the shooting, McKinley was not
getting better. He had developed an infection and was dying,

the telegram said. Roosevelt climbed down the mountain immediately. After a wild wagon ride through the night, he boarded a special train bound for Buffalo and McKinley's bedside. But he was too late. The president had died at 2:15 a.m.

Wearing a borrowed suit, his voice at first unsteady with emotion and nerves, Roosevelt took the oath of office in the home of a Buffalo lawyer. It was September 14, 1901. The country had a new president.

And what a president! Eager, boisterous, charming, charismatic, energetic, and interested in everything, Theodore Roosevelt had more energy at age 42 than most people do at any point in their lives. Everyone who met the 26th president remarked on his vibrancy. "You go to the White House, you shake hands with Roosevelt and hear him talk—and then you go home to wring the personality out of your clothes," a visitor once said. Roosevelt seized life and devoured it—books, sports, ideas, conversation, people. "By George," he once declared, "I don't believe I ever do talk with a man five minutes without liking him very much, unless I disliked him very much."

Roosevelt's appearance was as striking as his personality. He had a big barrel chest, a bristly mustache, and lots of teeth.

He was terribly nearsighted. When he fought as a soldier in Cuba, he had 12 pairs of eyeglasses sewn into his hat and clothes. Political cartoonists of the day wasted no time drawing caricatures.

Roosevelt was well aware that he had not been voted into the presidency, and yet he needed to govern. "It is a dreadful thing to come into the presidency this way," he wrote to his good friend Senator Henry Cabot Lodge. "But it would be a far worse thing to be morbid about it. Here is the task, and I have got to do it to the best of my ability; and that is all there is about it." Roosevelt knew he had to govern carefully and restore the

William McKinley (left) was only six months into his second term in office when he died, meaning Roosevelt served almost all of McKinley's four-year term.

public's trust in the stability of the U.S. government.

The president had just been assassinated, after all, and the country was shaken. The big hearty man in the White House had a knack for instilling confidence, though. In the first uncertain period of Roosevelt's presidency, he made it clear that he would follow in McKinley's footsteps. He purposely made no decisions that the Republican Party in power would not approve of.

Roosevelt had a hefty task ahead of him. He had inherited a country quickly rising to power as an industrial leader. He wanted to focus on promoting manufacturing and shipping, but he also faced serious problems. After the Civil War a small group of businessmen had made a huge amount of money owning and controlling railroad shipping, oil, and manufacturing. This small group controlled a lot of the money and power in the United States. An entire industry could be dominated by combinations of companies, called trusts. This practice hampered smaller companies not included in the trusts. They couldn't compete by offering lower prices. The trusts had the

Roosevelt's speeches are considered by historians to be some of the best of the 20th century.

power to decide supply routes and prices, which meant that the public was at their mercy.

Trusts were technically illegal. In 1890 Congress had passed the Sherman Antitrust Act, which prohibited trusts that restrained trade. But no one was challenging the trusts or enforcing the law. Determined to protect the public good, Roosevelt faced the business trusts head-on. He had to strike a balance between breaking up the trusts—trust-busting—while at the same time not stopping businesses from growing and thriving. In his annual message to Congress in 1901, Roosevelt declared, "The old laws, and the old customs ... were once quite sufficient to regulate the accumulation and distribution of wealth. Since the industrial changes which have so enormously increased the productive power of mankind, they are no longer sufficient."

Roosevelt's interest in trust-busting coexisted with new political movements that were becoming quite popular. Originating in the 1890s, reformers sought to help the poor and protect the rights of the common people. Roosevelt identified strongly with the reformers' goals, which included exposing the links between politicians and corrupt businessmen. These values shaped the way he dealt with the trusts.

In one of the first major actions of his term, Roosevelt focused on breaking up Northern Securities, a giant trust. Northern Securities dominated and controlled virtually all the railroads from Chicago to the Pacific Northwest. Roosevelt ordered the Justice Department to take action against Northern Securities for violating the Sherman Antitrust Act.

Business titan J. P. Morgan, one of the company's owners, was shocked that the law was being enforced. He and his associates were used to more private, "gentleman-to-gentleman" dealings. He should have been warned about the government's action, Morgan complained. But Roosevelt saw himself as a servant to the public, not to the wealthy business world. He was in office to protect the public's interests, and that was what he intended to do.

Roosevelt soon faced another test of his policies concerning the role of the government in business. In May 1902 about 140,000 coal miners went on strike. At a time when virtually

Political cartoons of the time often commented on Roosevelt's antitrust work. A Chicago Tribune cartoon depicted Roosevelt's "club" threatening a group of men labeled as various types of trusts and economic problems.

NEXT ON THE WAITING LIST OF THE ROOSEVELT CLUB

all homes were heated with coal, this event had the potential to become a major crisis. But the miners were desperate. They worked 12-hour days, six days a week. Their pay had been far outstripped by the cost of living, and much of their wages went to pay their debts at company stores. The miners were already unionized, but now they decided that it was time to strike.

The mine operators included railroad companies that carried coal to all parts of the country. The operators had no intention of changing wages or conditions or negotiating with the miners. The strike went on through the spring and summer, and the president watched from a distance.

But as winter approached, the nation's stockpile of coal dwindled. Americans were starting to panic about a winter without fuel to heat their homes. He needed to step in, the president decided. The government traditionally did not intervene in labor strikes, but this was different, Roosevelt thought. The strike not only affected the workers and mine operators. It was beginning to affect the general public. "The operators forget that they have duties toward the public, as well as rights to be guarded by the public through its governmental agents," Roosevelt wrote to his friend Robert Bacon. Some private businesses, Roosevelt concluded, were necessary for

Coal miners at the turn of the 20th century worked
in dirty and dangerous conditions.

society to keep functioning. They existed for the good of the
public and had to be run as such.

Stepping in carefully, Roosevelt opened talks between the
operators and the union. He convinced the mine operators
to accept the decision of an independent commission. The
operators reluctantly agreed. The commission decided terms to
end the strike, granting the miners some of their demands.

The president and the country breathed a sigh of relief.
The coal strike was over. And Roosevelt's conviction that
governments should oversee corporations, and be willing to
intervene if necessary, was solidified. He knew his first priority
must always be the welfare of the people.

FROM TEEDIE TO TEDDY

A stranger shown a picture of Theodore Roosevelt as a child would barely have recognized the hearty president. Born October 27, 1858, Teedie, as he was called, spent most of his first 12 years sick, nearsighted, and asthmatic. But Teedie was lucky in many other ways. Born into a very wealthy New York family, Teedie was interested in everything, especially nature and the outdoors. He read every book he could get his hands on. His asthma attacks lessened as he grew older, and soon scrawny little Teedie was a robust young man.

Roosevelt entered Harvard University at age 18. He quickly proved himself a natural leader. He met Alice Lee in 1878, and they married October 27, 1880. Roosevelt joined local politics and was elected to the New York State Assembly. But soon tragedy struck. Alice died February 14, 1884, two days after giving birth to their daughter, Alice. Roosevelt's mother died the same day, in the same house, of typhoid fever.

Roosevelt was devastated by grief. He fled to the West. After spending much of the next two years as a cowboy and ranch owner, he returned East. He married his childhood best friend, Edith Carow. He and Edith would have five children. President William McKinley appointed Roosevelt assistant secretary of the navy in 1897. Under Roosevelt's active leadership, the navy was ready for conflict when the Spanish-American War broke out.

Roosevelt was appointed to lead a group of soldiers the public nicknamed the Rough Riders into battle in Cuba. They achieved spectacular success on the battlefield in the Battle of San Juan Hill. That same year, 1898, Roosevelt was elected governor of New York, serving two years. He then was nominated as the Republican Party's candidate for vice president. He served six months as McKinley's vice president before being vaulted into the presidential office.

After he left office in 1909, Roosevelt was full of energy at age 50. He went on a safari to British East Africa and toured Europe. In 1912 he unsuccessfully ran for president again. Roosevelt died January 6, 1919. He was 60 years old.

International
SUCCESSES

Most would agree that Theodore Roosevelt's first unelected

term had been a success. But now he was facing the 1904

election, and the country would get to decide whether

they wanted the big man back in the White House for four

more years.

Unfortunately, Roosevelt could not attack his presidential

campaign in his natural, all-out style. Incumbent presidents did

not overtly campaign during Roosevelt's day—it was considered

unseemly. Roosevelt, an energetic and fiery speech maker, had

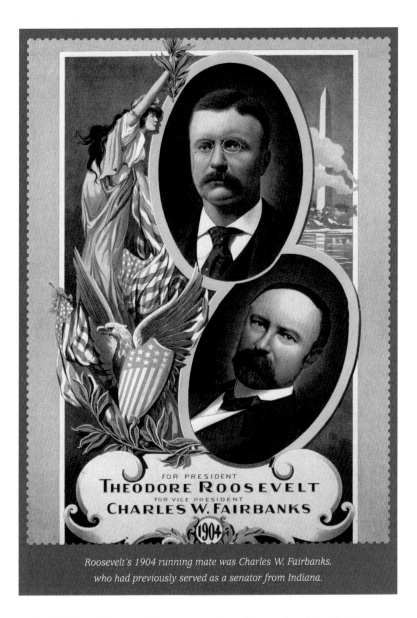

Roosevelt's 1904 running mate was Charles W. Fairbanks, who had previously served as a senator from Indiana.

to limit himself to sending out emissaries and writing letters. The president was accepting of his fate. "If elected I shall be very glad," he wrote to the author Rudyard Kipling. "If beaten I shall be very sorry; but in any event I have had a first class run for my money, and I have accomplished certain definite things."

Roosevelt was inaugurated and gave a speech March 4, 1905.

The nation was at peace, the economy stable. The incumbent was unhampered by dull Democratic nominee Alton B. Parker. Roosevelt swept the election and roared into the White House for his second term and his first term elected in his own right.

After the election Roosevelt felt at last that he had his mandate to govern. He was no longer an accidental president. He plunged right into his second term by pushing reforms.

DINNER AT THE WHITE HOUSE

During Roosevelt's day, racism was still rampant and commonplace. For the most part, white people kept the races separate and discriminated against black people, especially in the South. Slavery and the Civil War were only one generation removed, and many former slaves were still living. Roosevelt generally supported African-American rights.

So when the president wanted to discuss some government jobs in the southern states, he invited the prominent black educator Booker T. Washington to the White House. Washington dined with the president and first lady on October 16, 1901. They talked about politics, and Washington left around 10:00 p.m.

But the press soon heard that a black man had dined with the president, and a storm erupted. The southern newspapers were furious. More quietly, black activists hoped the dinner signaled some sympathy from the president in the face of the discrimination they confronted daily.

For his part, the president was shocked by the controversy. He wrote in a letter to Albion Tourgee, a U.S. diplomat, saying, "I respect [Booker T. Washington] greatly and believe in the work he has done. I have consulted so much with him it seemed to me that it was natural to ask him to dinner to talk over this work ... I do not intend to offend the prejudices of any one else, but neither do I intend to allow their prejudices to make me false to my principles."

Roosevelt mourned the state of race relations in the country. He continued to host black people at his private home in Oyster Bay, but Roosevelt was still a politician, and he wanted to seek re-election in 1904. He did not want to offend the South. Washington was never invited back to dine at the White House.

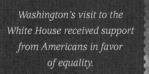

Washington's visit to the White House received support from Americans in favor of equality.

Politicians running for office were too closely linked to corporations, often being fed money and favors by businessmen who were hoping to win favors in return. Roosevelt proposed a law to Congress that corporations could not contribute to political campaigns. This election reform bill was so bold that it did not pass until 1907.

But Roosevelt liked to dream big. And almost since he had taken office in 1901, one dream had centered on a thin strip of land connecting North and South America.

American leaders had long desired a seaway through the isthmus that connected the two Americas. In those days before planes, a trip between New York and California by ship required sailing around the tip of South America, a journey of 13,000 miles (21,000 kilometers). And with the U.S. acquiring new territories and rising as a major world power, a canal through the isthmus would allow naval ships to swiftly maneuver back and forth between the Atlantic and Pacific coasts, potentially saving months of travel. The French had begun building a passage as far back as the 1880s, but the project had stalled.

Roosevelt was determined to build this canal. Colombia owned the land around the planned canal. Negotiations between the countries were slow. After a complicated and

Roosevelt (seated in steam shovel) became the first president to travel outside the U.S. while in office when he visited Panama in 1906.

messy series of diplomatic events, Roosevelt's chance finally came in 1903. A brand-new country, Panama, officially declared its independence from Colombia. Panama swiftly signed a treaty awarding the United States a 10-mile (16 km) strip of ground: the site of the future Panama Canal.

From the beginning, the engineering challenges were massive, unlike any faced before. There were mountains to blast, swamps to drain, and deadly diseases—malaria and yellow fever—to overcome. The leaders Roosevelt appointed each moved the canal toward completion, but after three years, the project reached a roadblock. The chief engineer,

John Stevens, resigned, leaving a still-chaotic organization.

But Roosevelt was undaunted. He found the perfect solution: putting the U.S. Army in charge. The army was used to big, long projects involving many men. Engineers led by Colonel George Goethals went to work. The canal was completed in 1914, a year ahead of schedule, with no scandals or corruption, and under budget.

Roosevelt was proving himself an effective leader in international affairs as well. Russia and Japan had been locked in conflict for two years, beginning in 1904. Roosevelt sought to preserve a balance of power in that unstable part of the world, and he had his eye on this potentially explosive situation. In an unprecedented initiative for an American president, Roosevelt invited Japanese and Russian representatives to discuss peace negotiations.

The Japanese and Russian diplomats met on August 9, 1905, in Portsmouth, New Hampshire. But the talks were uneasy. Each side was ready to bolt if Roosevelt showed favor to the other. But Roosevelt was ready. He invited both sides to lunch on the presidential yacht and counted on his personality and people skills to carry him through. Roosevelt escorted the leaders of both delegations into the yacht dining room so neither group could tell who entered first—a traditional matter

of importance to diplomats. Instead of a formal meal, he served

a buffet lunch from a round table. Everyone ate standing up.

That way, neither side would have a better seat and no one

would be served first. The meal was a success, and the peace

talks continued.

But trouble was also brewing elsewhere in the world—

trouble that could have threatened world peace. France and

A 1905 political cartoon depicts Roosevelt making peace between the Japanese and the Russians.

Roosevelt maintained good relations with Kaiser Wilhelm after his presidency, visiting the kaiser during his 1910 tour of Europe.

Germany were facing off over Morocco, which France was trying to establish as a French colony. The Germans did not want the French to increase their empire. With Great Britain supporting the French, the rising tension could have launched Europe into war.

Roosevelt stepped in once again, breaking with the previous American tradition of not intervening in European problems. Using some of the same tactics he had used with the Russians and Japanese, he participated in peace talks between the two sides. Over the voices of critics who cried that the United States had no interest in Morocco, peace talks began in Spain in 1906. Roosevelt focused on delicately handling Kaiser Wilhelm, Germany's leader. An uneasy peace prevailed.

Roosevelt's extraordinary diplomatic skills and his willingness to negotiate on behalf of other countries did not go unnoticed. In 1906 he was awarded the Nobel Peace Prize, the first American to win a Nobel prize in any category. Roosevelt was humble and gracious in his acceptance telegram. "I thank you on behalf of the United States," he wrote. "For what I did, I was able to accomplish only as the representative of the nation of which, for the time being, I am president."

Chapter Three

Decisions and
CONSEQUENCES

Even as a little boy, Theodore Roosevelt was fascinated by the natural world. He kept records of his nature observations and studied birds and insects on his own. He loved reading adventures of the outdoor life too. When his first wife died and he fled to the American West, his love for the outdoors crystallized into a full-on passion. But Roosevelt's love for the outdoors was not one of simple joy of observation. He appreciated nature—and was a widely recognized authority on birds—but he also realized and supported nature's role in

Roosevelt, who posed in his outdoor gear in 1885 at about age 27, is often called the "conservation president."

providing wealth and goods for people. Roosevelt was an avid hunter who took regular trips into the backcountry to shoot big game, such as elk, cougars, lynx, and bears. He promoted mining, logging, and damming rivers, all aimed toward distributing these resources among the general public.

After his 1904 election, Roosevelt felt that at last he had a mandate to advocate for the conservation of natural resources and the protection of the American environment. At the

A COWBOY AT HEART

Roosevelt spent time as a cowboy, hunter, and ranch owner in the West when he was in his 20s. He reveled in the rough life of the Dakota Badlands and never lacked adventure. In this letter written to his close friend Henry Cabot Lodge in 1886, Roosevelt describes hunting down three horse thieves:

"I got the three horse-thieves in fine style. My two Maine men and I ran down the river three days in our boat, and then came on their camp by surprise ... [T]hey were taken completely unawares, one with his rifle on the ground, and the others with theirs on their shoulders; so there was no fight, nor any need of pluck on our part. We simply crept noiselessly up and ... covered them with the cocked rifles while I told them to throw up their hands. They saw that we had the drop on them completely, and I guess they also saw that we surely meant shooting if they hesitated, and so their hands went up at once. We kept them with us nearly a week, being caught in an ice-jam; then we came to a ranch where I got a wagon, and ... I took the three captives overland a two days' journey to a town where I could give them to the sheriff. I was pretty sleepy when I got there, as I had to keep awake at night a good deal in guarding, and we had gotten out of food and the cold had been intense."

time vast swathes of American land, especially in the West, remained unsettled by white people. The Native American nations who had inhabited those lands for centuries still lived there, on their native soil. The "Indian Wars" in which settlers and the American government tried to forcibly remove Native Americans from their homeland had been taking place for more than 100 years. These conflicts were still going on, though they would draw to a close in the next 20 years.

Roosevelt (left) met conservationist John Muir in 1903 in Yosemite Valley in California. Muir fought for more public lands to be protected as parks.

With sharp foresight, Roosevelt could see that as the last frontier of the West was settled by whites, Americans' natural resources and wild spaces would be destroyed. Animals that were once common could become scarce. Roosevelt made preserving these "unsettled" lands a priority—within reason. "Conservation means development as much as it does protection," he stated in a speech in Kansas in 1910. "I recognize the right and duty of this generation to develop and

June 21, 1902.

My dear Mr. Bixby:

Will you please talk with Mr. Gifford Pinchot over
a possible forest reserve in Indian Territory? As you
know, I am greatly interested in forest reserves.

Sincerely yours,

Theodore Roosevelt

Roosevelt took advantage of every opportunity to preserve parkland. He instructs Tams Bixby, a government official in Oklahoma Territory, to talk about forest preservation with Gifford Pinchot, the first head of the U.S. Forest Service.

use the natural resources of our land but I do not recognize the right to waste them, or to rob, by wasteful use, the generations that come after us ..."

With this goal in mind, Roosevelt established the U.S. Forest Service, which protects and maintains forestlands. Protected forests increased from 42 million acres (17 million hectares) to 172 million acres (69.6 million hectares) under Roosevelt's administration. He created 51 national wildlife refuges and five national parks.

Roosevelt was also careful to ensure that the land was useful to the people—though that carefulness extended mostly to white people. Native Americans, Roosevelt sincerely believed, held no claim to the land they inhabited, especially if they were nomadic rather than settled in one place. Since Abraham Lincoln's presidency in the 1860s, homesteaders willing to settle certain areas had received free land grants. Roosevelt continued this practice and signed a law increasing the amount of acreage granted to settlers from 160 acres (65 hectares) to 320 acres (130 hectares). He wanted the land used but not destroyed or stripped of its wealth and beauty.

Roosevelt helped solidify permanent government protection of natural resources in 1906 when he signed the Antiquities Act.

Theodore Roosevelt National Park in North Dakota, named for the president, protects rugged land and a wide variety of wildlife.

This far-reaching act, which is still in use today, gave presidents the power to protect important natural areas in the country.

The president can withdraw federal lands from public use if that land contains "objects of historic, scenic or scientific significance." No other president before had taken such an active and innovative approach to land conservation.

Even before his second term, Roosevelt had been considering the problem of corruption in the railroad industry. In 1904 he began tackling the issue of unfairly set railroad rates. Farmers and business owners relied on railroads to ship their goods and produce all over the country. And the railroads knew how indispensible their services were. They raised the rates they charged again and again, often seeking kickbacks and securing favors, crushing small businesses. Roosevelt, always remembering his promise to protect the public good, decided

that this unfair practice had gone far enough. The railroad

companies and those who financed them had to be reined in.

He was taking action, Roosevelt explained to Congress, for

the same reason he had intervened in the coal strike of 1902.

Railroads were essential to public welfare and the commerce

of the country. In the United States, in Roosevelt's time as well

as today, the federal government does not generally interfere

with private business. This is one of the rules of capitalism, the

economic system under which the country operates. However,

A 1902 Washington Post *story and cartoon about Roosevelt's refusal to shoot a chained bear in Mississippi led to his association with the toy teddy bear.*

Roosevelt understood how critical rail transportation was for the country at the beginning of the 20th century.

this low interference approach is not absolute. Businesses are subject to regulation by the government and must conduct their business according to the law and in a fair manner.

Roosevelt certainly agreed that businesses were private enterprises and must be permitted to compete and set prices based on supply and demand. But he believed that exceptions could be made when the good of the public was at risk. And in this case, the railroads were not playing fair, he felt. "We should be as sure of the proper conduct of the interstate railways and the proper management of interstate business as we are now sure of the conduct and management of the national banks," Roosevelt said in a 1910 speech after leaving the presidency. "And we should have as effective supervision in one case as in the other."

Roosevelt felt encouraged by his win in the 1904 election. The railroad men, oilmen, and financiers who funneled his opponents money were powerful people, but riding high on the sails of his victory, Roosevelt was ready to tackle them. He spoke with both Republicans and Democrats. He explained that enacting some regulations was a good compromise between uncontrolled growth of the railroads and full government ownership of them—a philosophy Roosevelt had maintained throughout his career. He proposed the Hepburn Act, a law giving the Interstate Commerce Commission (ICC) more power to regulate the railroads and enforce the laws that bound them. The ICC would be able to set maximum shipping rates and could require railroads to submit annual reports of their financial accounts. But conservative senators in Congress balked. They did not want this added regulation. Roosevelt could have let the issue die. But instead, he decided to appeal directly to the American people, in hopes of convincing them to support the regulations. He went on a speaking tour across the western states. This was one of the first times a president actively used members of the press, who were covering him at every stop, to pressure Congress. And it worked. The issues were taken up, and in 1906 Congress passed the Hepburn Act.

Roosevelt tackled another serious threat to the public good at the same time that he was addressing railroad abuses. Prior to 1906 food and medicine production and sale were almost completely unregulated in the United States. Diseased animals were routinely slaughtered for meat. Poor working conditions in slaughterhouses caused worker injuries and deaths. Any unqualified person who wanted to manufacture something and call it "medicine" and sell it could also boast outrageous claims about its curing powers. But a group of muckraking journalists was investigating these practices and exposing them to the public.

One of these writers was Upton Sinclair, a socialist whose novel *The Jungle* described in stomach-turning detail the

You ask - "Is there anything further, say in the Department of Agriculture, which you would suggest my doing?" I would
suggest the following: That you do as Doubleday, Page & Company
did; find a man concerning whose intelligence and integrity you
are absolutely sure; send him up here, or let me meet him in
Washington, and tell him all that I saw, and how I saw it, and
give him the names and addresses of the people who will enable
him to see it. Then let him go to Packingtown as I did, as a work-
ing-man; live with the men, get a job in the yards, and use his
eyes and ears; and see if he does not come out at the end of a few
weeks feeling, as did the special correspondent of the London
"Lancet," whom I met in Chicago, that the conditions in the pack-
ing-houses constitute a "menace to the health of the civilized
world." *The Lancet for Jan 8, 15, 22, 29 — 1905.*

Thanking you for your kind interest,

Very sincerely,

Upton Sinclair

Upton Sinclair advised Roosevelt on what to do to reform food production.

revolting practices of the slaughterhouses and meatpacking
and pickling factories. Roosevelt read the book and was
shocked. He plunged into reforming the food safety system in
the country, focusing in particular on the role of government
inspectors. Once again, Roosevelt was determined to protect
the public good by extending government regulations. By 1906

Roosevelt signed the Pure Food and Drugs Act. It was the first time that consumers were given even basic protection from the dangers of unregulated foods and medicines. The law would later give rise to what we know today as the Food and Drug Administration.

But 1906 was not an entirely successful year for Roosevelt. In fact, he made what many consider to be the biggest mistake of his time in office—and it was over the question of race.

On the night of August 13, 1906, a shooting occurred in Brownsville, Texas. A white bartender was killed and a white police officer was wounded. Town officials blamed soldiers of the all-black 25th Infantry Regiment stationed nearby, although the unit's white commander said all the soldiers were in the fort at the time. The investigations were inconclusive, partly because the soldiers refused to talk to the police or military investigators. The U.S. Army was convinced of their guilt, and Roosevelt gave the whole regiment a dishonorable discharge. Some of the soldiers had served for years, and six had won the Medal of Honor.

Some accused Roosevelt of acting rashly, and some opponents were happy to accuse him of racism. Roosevelt's good friend Booker T. Washington told him he had made a

Roosevelt (circled, left) and Booker T. Washington appeared together in 1905 in Tuskegee, Alabama, before the events in Brownsville.

serious mistake. Other black leaders saw Roosevelt's actions as a step backward in race relations. Roosevelt remained unmoved, convinced of the rightness of his actions. Later, some soldiers were restored to duty.

Of Dollars
AND SHIPS

In late 1907 stock market values plunged by 37 percent.
Panic swept the country. No fan of Theodore Roosevelt's
regulations on business, Wall Street leapt at the chance to blame
the president's economic policies for the tumble. Roosevelt
rejected this charge. He believed that his policies of curbing
unregulated business had been good for the country. Later
economists point to a variety of causes for the drop, including
structural problems in the financial system and years of
uncontrolled economic growth.

The financial panic in 1907 caused a run on some banks, when people rushed to withdraw their money.

Whatever the cause the situation was growing worse. At least 25 banks would fail. The president gritted his teeth and faced the problem in his usual manner: head-on. He met with J. P. Morgan, the nation's most powerful banker. Morgan leaned on the big New York bankers and convinced them to combine their funds to rescue the failing banks. The federal government contributed a like sum to stabilize the economy and reassure investors. In the bargain, Morgan and his partners were assured that certain holdings would be exempt from antitrust prosecution. The crisis passed.

International issues held Roosevelt's attention as well throughout his second term. Roosevelt had enjoyed his job as assistant secretary of the navy and maintained his naval interest throughout his presidency. He studied ship weaponry and compared the United States ships with those of Germany and Japan. One of his dearest dreams was to build a navy that would compete with the most powerful in the world.

Cartoonists made fun of Roosevelt's relationship with powerful, wealthy men such as J. P. Morgan and Andrew Carnegie.

But Roosevelt's naval dreams were not just an indulgent personal interest. The world—particularly Japan and Germany—was becoming more dangerous, he argued, and the United States must be prepared to defend itself and even go on the offensive if necessary. Many members of Congress disagreed, preferring to focus on domestic programs. But World War I (1914–1918) was only a few years away. The United States would indeed need a mighty navy.

Roosevelt decided the U.S. should do something no country had ever done before: he proposed a global goodwill tour by naval vessels. He ordered a fleet of battleships painted white, and, in December 1907, the Great White Fleet left on a cruising mission around the world. Everyone would see how strong the U.S. Navy truly was.

Roosevelt's plan worked brilliantly. For 14 months the fleet of battleships and their smaller attendant ships sailed around the world. The shining white ships drew massive crowds at every port. When they at last sailed back to

IT'S A FACT

By the Numbers: The Great White Fleet

- **Battleships: 16, plus multiple support ships**

- **Sailors: 14,000**

- **Distance traveled: 43,000 miles (69,000 km)**

- **Ports visited: 20, on six continents**

The 16 battleships of the Great White Fleet were all less than 10 years old.

their Virginia port, spread out over 7 miles (11 km), Roosevelt welcomed them home jubilantly. "This morning the hearts of all who saw you thrilled with pride as the hulls of the mighty warships lifted above the horizon," Roosevelt told the admiral and his crew members. "As a war machine the fleet comes back in better shape than it went out. In addition, you, the officers and men of this formidable fighting force, have shown yourselves the best of all possible ambassadors and heralds of peace."

Though his presidency was drawing to a close, Roosevelt did not relent in his long crusade for his reform agenda.

During the last two years of his administration, he fought corruption where he found it and increased his demands on Congress. As he wrote in a 1907 letter, "One of the chief things I have tried to preach to the American politician, and the American businessman, is not to grasp at money, place, power, or enjoyment in any form, simply because he can probably get it, without regard to considerations of morality and national interest ..."

Roosevelt's list of demands for Congress was a long one. He wanted to strengthen regulation of interstate business, since individual states were unable to control between-state transactions. He wanted an inheritance tax and an income tax—both of which became law. He wanted an eight-hour workday for laborers, rather than the 14-hour day many worked at the time. He wanted to regulate the stock market so that the public would find investing in stocks as secure as opening a bank account. Roosevelt called his domestic agenda the Square Deal, because he tried to strike a balance between business

IT'S A FACT

When the Roosevelts entered the White House, the mansion was in such bad repair that Congress spent $540,000 to fix the structural beams, heating, electrical wiring, and pest infestations. It became a modern home for the leader of the country, one of which the nation could be proud.

Roosevelt's presidency did much to set up the course the country would take throughout the 20th century.

and consumers, laborers and those who managed them, and those who wanted to conserve land and those who wished to develop it.

Roosevelt did not get all of the demands he requested. But he got some of them, and much of his legacy lives today.

THE FAMILY BEHIND THE PRESIDENT

By all accounts, Roosevelt was a warm, active, and involved father to his six children, Alice, Theodore, Kermit, Ethel, Archie, and Quentin, all born between 1884 and 1897. He taught his four boys to ride, shoot, play ball games, and wrestle. Roosevelt never forgot how to play like a child. He was known to have to change his clothes before attending official White House functions because they were so covered in feathers from pillow fights. He frequently played hide-and-seek with his daughter Ethel and her friends in the White House attic. The president preferred to be "it."

The Roosevelt children were known for their antics. Once they took a pony up in the White House elevator to visit Archie when he was sick. And they maintained a menagerie of pets that included a hyena, a badger, and a small bear, in addition to many more common animals.

The public also took great interest in the activities of Roosevelt's daughter by his first wife. Seventeen when her father became president, Alice Lee was called Princess Alice by the press. She was a beauty with a love for the outrageous. She wore the most fashionable clothes, attended horse races, was rumored to carry a snake in her purse, smoked on the roof of the White House, and was always surrounded by male admirers. When asked at one point why he didn't control his wild daughter, Roosevelt replied that he could either be president or attend to Alice—but not do both at the same time.

Roosevelt shared his love of the outdoors with his family.

The Old
LION

After the 1904 election, Theodore Roosevelt declared that

he would not seek another term as president. Official term

limits did not yet exist, but presidents typically followed the

precedent set by George Washington and did not serve more

than two terms. Roosevelt declared he would abide by this even

though his first term was only partial. "The wise custom which

limits the President to two terms regards the substance and not

the form. Under no circumstances will I be a candidate for or

History considers William Howard Taft (right) a skilled lawyer and judge but a poor politician. He later served as chief justice of the United States on the Supreme Court.

accept another nomination," read a statement Roosevelt issued on election night.

Later Roosevelt would regret his decision. He was only 50 years old when he left office in 1908 and still bursting with energy. Moreover, he genuinely enjoyed the job of president, unlike many before and after him. But Roosevelt had said he would not run and he meant to keep his word.

William Howard Taft, secretary of war, was the man Roosevelt wanted to succeed him. The portly, amiable former judge from Cincinnati, Ohio, had been a close aide and friend for many years. Roosevelt believed that Taft would support the progressive policies he had so carefully crafted throughout his administration.

The election went smoothly. Roosevelt was popular and he had chosen an inoffensive man, so Taft won easily. Confident he had chosen correctly, Roosevelt went off on a safari to East Africa, accompanied by 260 porters, more than 50 classic books, nine pairs of eyeglasses, four tons (3.6 metric tons) of salt to cure animal hides, and his son Kermit. He and his team spent a year shooting an astonishing 11,000 vertebrates, including 5,000 mammals. Roosevelt and Kermit together killed

Roosevelt's safari in Africa combined his passions of scientific inquiry and hunting.

512 animals. These facts might seem appalling to modern readers, but Roosevelt's safari was sponsored by both the Smithsonian and the American Museum of Natural History. Every specimen was meticulously noted and was preserved for study or display, except when providing food for the group. Many species were previously unknown. Many of Roosevelt's captures are still on display in museums.

After leaving Africa and touring Europe, the still enormously popular former president arrived back in the U.S. to upsetting news. Taft was not doing well as president. His policies toward trusts and tariffs were inconsistent and had unsettled the economy. And Taft reversed or violated many of Roosevelt's conservation policies.

The beginning of a split between Taft and Roosevelt had begun. It deepened when Roosevelt gave the most important speech of his post-presidential career in Osawatomie, Kansas, on August 31, 1910.

"At many stages in the advance of humanity," Roosevelt declared, "this conflict between the men who possess more than they have earned and the men who have earned more than they possess is the central condition of progress. In our day it appears as the struggle of freemen to gain and hold the right of self-government as against the special interests, who twist the methods of free government into machinery for defeating the popular will. At every stage, and under all circumstances, the essence of the struggle is to equalize opportunity, destroy privilege, and give to the life and citizenship of every individual the highest possible value both to himself and to the commonwealth."

Roosevelt was advocating a political doctrine that he called New Nationalism—in essence, it included the more progressive views he had always held, especially during the last years of his presidency. His opinions alarmed the conservative side of his Republican Party (which included Taft), while at the same time energizing his reform-minded followers, then called Insurgents.

But when Roosevelt's friends expressed surprise and horror at his supposedly radical ideas, Roosevelt himself was surprised. He insisted that these ideas—income and inheritance taxes that increased with a person's wealth; government supervision of trusts; workmen's compensation; and regulation of child labor, to name just a few—were the same ones he had always advocated.

Despite initially insisting he was out of politics, Roosevelt decided to run for president in 1912. Taft's administration

Roosevelt greeted supporters during the 1912 election campaign.

claimed that Roosevelt had been hoodwinked by J. P. Morgan in the 1907 banking crisis. This and other betrayals of Roosevelt's policies and Taft's promises led Roosevelt and a large number of Republicans to oppose the sitting president. However, the so-called boss system, in which powerful figures exerted influence on candidates, showed its power. Despite winning more states and primary delegates than Taft, Roosevelt watched as boss control of the presidential convention, and controversial delegate selection, gave the nomination to Taft.

DESPITE A BULLET

The old Rough Rider displayed his legendary toughness in October 1912 when he was shot in the chest after leaving his hotel and greeting a crowd on his way to an election rally in Milwaukee, Wisconsin. The bullet pierced Roosevelt's eyeglass case and a folded 50-page manuscript of a speech in his breast pocket before lodging near his rib. Roosevelt was not undone, however.

He concluded that since he was not spitting blood, the bullet hadn't pierced his lung. He gave his speech at the rally, speaking for an hour and a half, before allowing himself to be removed to the hospital. He told the crowd it would take more than one bullet to stop a bull moose. The shooter, John Schrank, reportedly said he did it because no one should be president three times.

Roosevelt and his supporters broke with the Republicans and formed their own party—the National Progressive Party, also called the Bull Moose Party. It was named after their impressive leader, who declared that he felt as strong as a "bull moose." Roosevelt went head-to-head during the campaign with Taft and the dry, severe Woodrow Wilson, the Democratic nominee.

Wilson beat Roosevelt, but Roosevelt prevailed over Taft. The president, in fact, won only two states.

The still-vigorous Roosevelt accepted his defeat and retreated back into the arms of his family at Sagamore Hill, his New York home. Through the next seven years, he wrote his autobiography, took part in a river expedition in Brazil, wrote

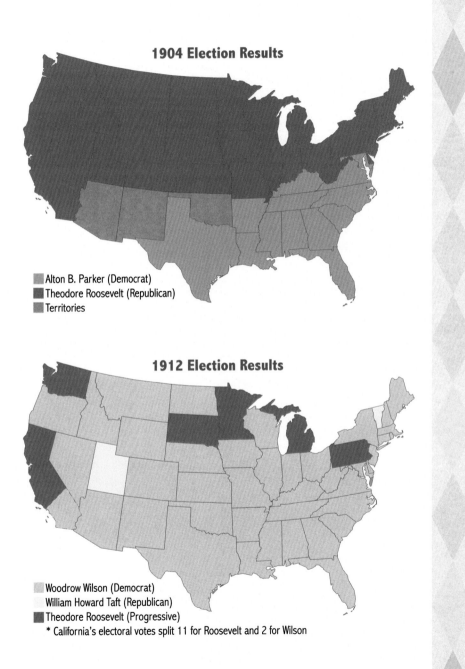

1904 Election Results

Alton B. Parker (Democrat)
Theodore Roosevelt (Republican)
Territories

1912 Election Results

Woodrow Wilson (Democrat)
William Howard Taft (Republican)
Theodore Roosevelt (Progressive)
* California's electoral votes split 11 for Roosevelt and 2 for Wilson

articles, and gave speeches. In 1918 Roosevelt's youngest son Quentin died in World War I when his plane was shot down. Roosevelt never recovered from his son's death.

Just six months after Quentin's death, 60-year-old Roosevelt, in failing health, died of a type of blood clot called an embolism. One of his sons sent a telegram with the news to his brothers fighting overseas in World War I. It read, "The old lion is dead."

Roosevelt's legacy is still strong in the 21st century. Every time a modern American takes a bite of safe meat, reads the label on a bottle of pills, chooses between competing companies, or visits one of many national parks, he or she is reaping the benefits of Roosevelt's tireless work on behalf of those he always strove to protect: the American public.

Theodore Roosevelt

TIMELINE

1858
Theodore Roosevelt is born October 27 in New York City to Theodore and Martha Roosevelt

1880
Roosevelt marries Alice Lee on October 27 in Massachusetts

1898
Roosevelt leads the Rough Riders into battle in Cuba during the Spanish-American War; he is elected governor of New York

1897
Roosevelt is appointed assistant secretary of the navy by President William McKinley on April 19

1901
Roosevelt takes office as vice president March 4 under President William McKinley; Roosevelt becomes president when McKinley dies September 14

1905
Roosevelt creates the United States Forest Service; he moderates peace talks between the Japanese and Russian governments

1907
Roosevelt works to avert financial panic after the economic plunge; the Great White Fleet leaves for a worldwide cruise in December

1881
Roosevelt is elected to the New York State Assembly as a Republican

1884
Alice Lee gives birth to a daughter, Alice, and dies two days later, February 14; Roosevelt's mother dies the same day; in June, Roosevelt flees New York for the Dakota Territory

1886
Roosevelt marries his childhood friend Edith Kermit Carow on December 2

1903
Roosevelt creates the first national wildlife refuge; land is secured for construction of the Panama Canal

1904
Roosevelt wins his first presidential election in his own right by a landslide and pledges not to seek another term

1912
Roosevelt loses the campaign for president to Woodrow Wilson, running second, ahead of President Taft

1909
William Howard Taft is inaugurated in March; Roosevelt leaves for an East African safari

1919
Roosevelt dies in his sleep from an embolism January 6 at his home, Sagamore Hill, in New York

GLOSSARY

anarchist—someone who wants to overturn and dismantle government

caricature—a picture that shows the defects or qualities of a person in an exaggerated manner

fleet—a group of warships under one command

incumbent—the present holder of an office

isthmus—a narrow strip of land that has water on both sides and connects two larger sections of land

mandate—the authorization to act a certain way or on a certain issue, given to an elected official by the public

muckraking—searching for and exposing corruption and scandal

socialist—follower of an economic system in which the government owns most businesses

strike—to refuse to work because of a disagreement with the employer over wages or working conditions

trust—separate companies that join to limit competition by controlling production and distribution of products and services

unionized—formed into an organization of workers in order to deal collectively with employers

ADDITIONAL RESOURCES

FURTHER READING

Cooper, Michael L. *Theodore Roosevelt: A Twentieth-Century Life.* New York: Viking, 2009.

Harness, Cheryl. *The Remarkable Rough-Riding Life of Theodore Roosevelt and the Rise of Empire America.* Washington, D.C.: National Geographic, 2007.

Marrin, Albert. *The Great Adventure: Theodore Roosevelt and the Rise of Modern America.* New York: Dutton Children's Books, 2007.

INTERNET SITES

Use FactHound to find Internet sites related to this book. All of the sites on FactHound have been researched by our staff.

Here's all you do:

Visit *www.facthound.com*

Type in this code: 9780756549251

CRITICAL THINKING USING THE COMMON CORE

Theodore Roosevelt caused a controversy when he invited the African-American educator Booker T. Washington to a meal at the White House. Roosevelt supported black people in their struggle for equality, but he never repeated his invitation after receiving heavy criticism. Do you agree or disagree with Roosevelt's actions in this case? What could have been the consequences, positive or negative, if Roosevelt had invited Washington or other black leaders back to dine at the White House? *(Integration of Knowledge and Ideas)*

Roosevelt enjoyed being president. Why did he refuse to seek a third consecutive term? How did this decision affect the specific political choices he made afterward? *(Key Ideas and Details)*

Roosevelt left the United States many legacies—the expansion of national parks and protected wilderness, regulation of businesses, and a safer food and drug supply, to name just a few. What do you think is Roosevelt's greatest legacy? Why? *(Integration of Knowledge and Ideas)*

SOURCE NOTES

Page 6, line 14: Edmund Morris. *Theodore Rex*. New York: Modern Library, 2001, p. xxxi.

Page 6, line 18: Edward Wagenknecht. *The Seven Worlds of Theodore Roosevelt*. Guilford, Conn.: Lyons Press, 2009, p. 127.

Page 7, line 6: H. W. Brands. *American Colossus: The Triumph of Capitalism, 1865–1900*, New York: Doubleday, 2010, p. 546.

Page 9, line 11: Mario R. DiNunzio, ed. *Theodore Roosevelt: An American Mind, Selected Writings*. New York: Penguin Books, 1994, p. 127.

Page 12, line 18: Paul Rego. *American Ideal: Theodore Roosevelt's Search for American Individualism*. Lanham, Md.: Lexington Books, 2008, p. 117.

Page 17, line 2: Louis Auchincloss, ed. *Theodore Roosevelt: Letters and Speeches*. New York: Literary Classics of the United States, 2004, p. 358.

Page 19, line 19: *Theodore Roosevelt: Letters and Speeches*, pp. 244–245.

Page 25, line 14: "The Nobel Peace Prize 1906: Theodore Roosevelt Acceptance Speech." Nobelprize.org. 6 Feb. 2014. http://www.nobelprize.org/nobel_prizes/peace/laureates/1906/roosevelt-acceptance.html

Page 28 sidebar, line 11: *Theodore Roosevelt: Letters and Speeches*, p. 20.

Page 29, line 6: Ibid., p. 808.

Page 32, line 5: "The Antiquities Act: Protecting America's National Heritage." National Parks Conservation Association Fact Sheet. 6 Feb. 2014. http://www.npca.org/news/media-center/fact-sheets/2013-Antiquities-Act-fact-sheet.pdf

Page 35, line 3: *Theodore Roosevelt: Letters and Speeches*, p. 805.

Page 44, line 2: Theodore Roosevelt. *Theodore Roosevelt: An Autobiography*. New York: Charles Scribner's Sons, 1925, pp. 557–558.

Page 45, line 6: *Theodore Roosevelt: Letters and Speeches*, p. 540.

Page 48, line 6: *Theodore Roosevelt: An Autobiography*. p. 387.

Page 51, line 18: *Theodore Roosevelt: Letters and Speeches*, pp. 802–803.

Page 54, line 5: "Today in History: June 22: Bull Moose Born." The Library of Congress American Memory. 6 Feb. 2014. http://memory.loc.gov/ammem/today/jun22.html

Page 56, line 7: Nathan Miller. *Theodore Roosevelt: A Life*. New York: William Morrow, 1992, p. 566.

SELECT BIBLIOGRAPHY

"American President: Theodore Roosevelt." The Miller Center University of Virginia. http://millercenter.org/president/roosevelt/essays/biography/4

"The Antiquities Act: Protecting America's National Heritage." National Parks Conservation Association Fact Sheet. http://www.npca.org/news/media-center/fact-sheets/2013-Antiquities-Act-fact-sheet.pdf

Auchincloss, Louis. *The American Presidents Series: Theodore Roosevelt*. New York: Henry Holt, 2001.

Auchincloss, Louis, ed. *Theodore Roosevelt: Letters and Speeches*. New York: Literary Classics of the United States, 2004.

Barber, James G. *Theodore Roosevelt: Icon of the American Century*. Washington, D.C.: Smithsonian Institution, 1998.

Davis, Deborah. *Guest of Honor: Booker T. Washington, Theodore Roosevelt, and the White House Dinner That Shocked a Nation*. New York: Atria Books, 2012.

DiNunzio, Mario R., ed. *Theodore Roosevelt: An American Mind, Selected Writings*. New York: Penguin Books, 1994.

Donald, Aida D. *Lion in the White House: A Life of Theodore Roosevelt*. New York: Basic Books, 2007.

"Hepburn Act." The Theodore Roosevelt Center at Dickinson State University. http://www.theodorerooseveltcenter.org/en/Learn-About-TR/TR-Encyclopedia/Capitalism-and-Labor/The-Hepburn-Act.aspx

Marschall, Rick. *Bully: The Life and Times of Theodore Roosevelt*. Washington, D.C.: Regnery History, 2011.

Miller, Nathan. *Theodore Roosevelt: A Life*. New York: William Morrow, 1992.

Morris, Edmund. *The Rise of Theodore Roosevelt*. New York: Random House, 1979.

"The Nobel Peace Prize 1906: Theodore Roosevelt Acceptance Speech." Nobelprize.org. http://www.nobelprize.org/nobel_prizes/peace/laureates/1906/roosevelt-acceptance.html

Roosevelt, Theodore. *Theodore Roosevelt: An Autobiography*. New York: Charles Scribner's Sons, 1925.

"Sherman Anti-Trust Act (1890)." U.S. National Archives and Records Administration. http://www.ourdocuments.gov/doc.php?flash=true&doc=51

"Theodore Roosevelt and the Panama Canal." PBS: American Experience. http://www.pbs.org/wgbh/americanexperience/features/general-article/tr-panama/

"Today in History: June 22: Bull Moose Born." The Library of Congress American Memory. http://memory.loc.gov/ammem/today/jun22.html

INDEX

ABOUT THE AUTHOR

Emma Carlson Berne has written numerous
historical and biographical books for children and
young adults, as well as young adult fiction. She
lives in Cincinnati with her husband and two sons.